SOCIAL SCIENCE

Spies of the American Revolution

MARCIA AMIDON LUSTED

TABLE OF CONTENTS

What Spies Do 2
American Patriots 4
The Culper Spy Ring 8
British Spies 12
Spy Women 16
Who Out-Spied Whom? 19
Glossary/Index 20

PIONEER VALLEY EDUCATIONAL PRESS, INC

WHAT SPIES DO

When the American colonies fought Britain for their independence during the Revolutionary War, spies on both sides made a significant impact in the conflict. These secret soldiers helped military leaders plan strategies, learn where **munitions** were stored, and discover where the enemy was headed. They then carried secret messages with this information to other military leaders, who used it to **thwart** attacks or overcome the enemy.

In some cases, spies purposely gave incorrect information to the other side. Posing as peddlers or runaway slaves, they told the enemy that troops were headed in one direction when they were really moving the other way. This helped them catch the enemy off guard.

>>> During colonial times, peddlers commonly moved from place to place to sell goods.

AMERICAN PATRIOTS

Benjamin Franklin was one of the best-known patriots and colonial leaders. Famous for his amazing inventions, he was also a spymaster for the American colonies. A spymaster controls all the spies working for an army. In addition to his other jobs, Benjamin served as one of the original members of the Committee of Secret Correspondence. He also ran a network of spies in France.

MORE TO EXPLORE

The **CENTRAL INTELLIGENCE AGENCY** (CIA) now handles work that used to belong to the Committee of Secret Correspondence. The CIA collects, analyzes, and provides information to keep our country safe.

Nathan Hale was another famous American spy. After graduating from college, Nathan became a schoolteacher. When war broke out, he **enlisted** and eventually became a captain under George Washington. When Nathan learned that General Washington was looking for a volunteer to spy behind enemy lines, he decided to help the patriotic cause. His mission was to send reports about what British troops were doing. He disguised himself as a Dutch teacher looking for work, but according to legend, someone recognized him. The British captured Nathan and found sketches of British **fortifications** and detailed battle information in his shoes. He was executed as a spy in 1776.

Nathan's legendary last words were: "I only regret that I have but one life to lose for my country."

James Armistead Lafayette was an enslaved African American who joined the army in 1781 with the permission of his slaveholder. He worked as a **double agent** for the American army. Pretending to be a runaway slave, he offered to work for the British, but he was really collecting information about their army. His reports helped the Americans win at the Battle of Yorktown.

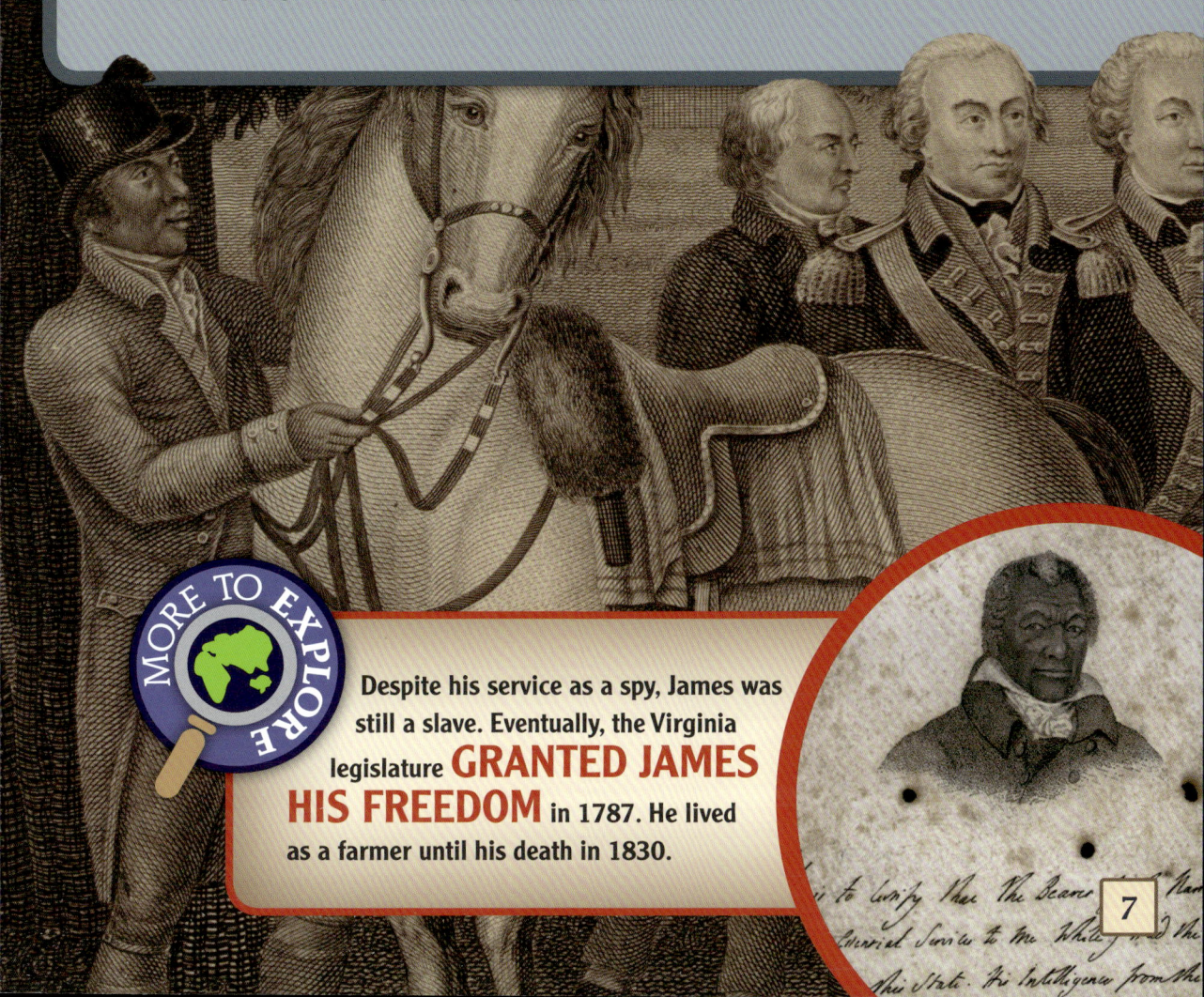

More to Explore

Despite his service as a spy, James was still a slave. Eventually, the Virginia legislature **GRANTED JAMES HIS FREEDOM** in 1787. He lived as a farmer until his death in 1830.

THE CULPER SPY RING

In August 1776, British forces occupied New York. George Washington was desperate for information about enemy troop movements, but there was no official group to provide the information he needed. That changed in 1778 when George made Major Benjamin Tallmadge the head of the Continental Army's secret service. As George's official spymaster, Benjamin established a spy network to operate behind British lines on Long Island, New York.

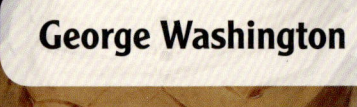

George Washington

8

Benjamin asked his childhood friends to be part of the spy ring. One of them was farmer Abraham Woodhull, who decided how messages would pass among the group and then to General Washington. Abraham also traveled back and forth to New York. He lived in constant fear of getting caught, so he recruited Robert Townsend, a New York merchant, to assist him. Abraham used the name Samuel Culper to hide his identity; Robert went by Samuel Culper Jr. This famed crew came to be known as the Culper Spy Ring.

Robert Townsend

Benjamin Tallmadge

Abraham Woodhull

In addition to using code names, members of the Culper Spy Ring used a **cipher system**, a code book, and invisible ink. They set up "dead drop" locations so one spy could drop off information and another could pick it up. They transported messages in empty eggshells and hollow bullets.

cylindrical cipher

Culper Ring code

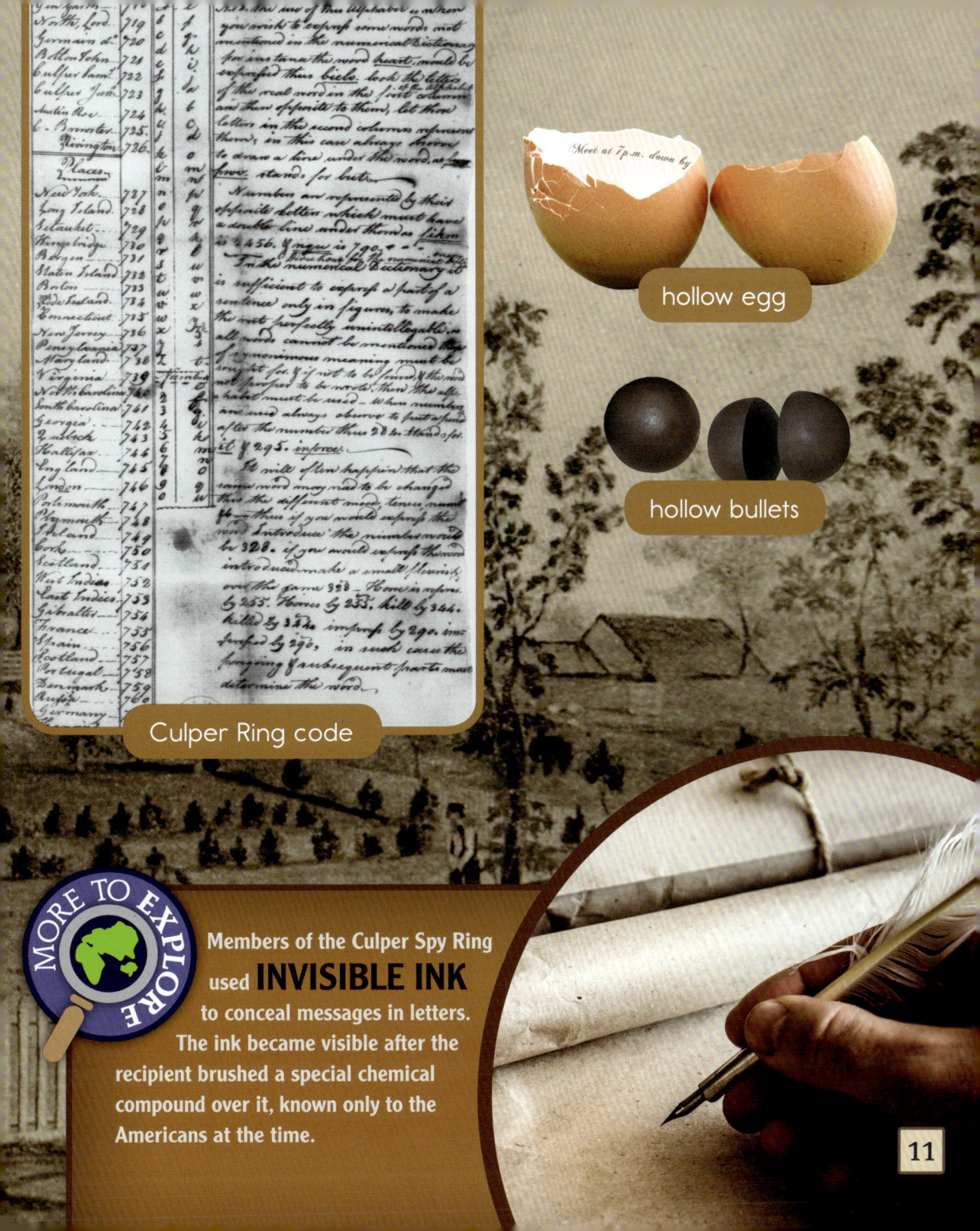

hollow egg

hollow bullets

MORE TO EXPLORE

Members of the Culper Spy Ring used **INVISIBLE INK** to conceal messages in letters. The ink became visible after the recipient brushed a special chemical compound over it, known only to the Americans at the time.

11

BRITISH SPIES

Not surprisingly, the enemy also had their own spies during the Revolutionary War. Benedict Arnold was a general in George Washington's army who helped win several important battles. But Benedict became angry when he was not promoted.

Benedict became a spy for the British and used secret messages to tell them where American troops were. How did he do it? Benedict's wife, Peggy, was loyal to the British. Benedict used invisible ink to add secret messages to Peggy's letters, then passed her notes to British commanders. Benedict also plotted to help the British seize the American fort at West Point, New York.

ONE OF THE TREASON LETTERS IN CYPHER

MORE TO EXPLORE

George Washington found out about Benedict and tried to capture him, but the spy and his family **ESCAPED TO ENGLAND**.

Benjamin Church was an incredibly dangerous British spy whom many people have never heard of. Benjamin was a member of many Massachusetts patriot groups and a doctor so well respected that he was appointed surgeon general of the American army. His high standing in Boston patriot circles and his work at the hospital gave him access to much military intelligence, which he passed on to the British. No one is sure why Benjamin became a spy, but perhaps his **lavish** lifestyle, spending habits, and British wife led him to become a traitor.

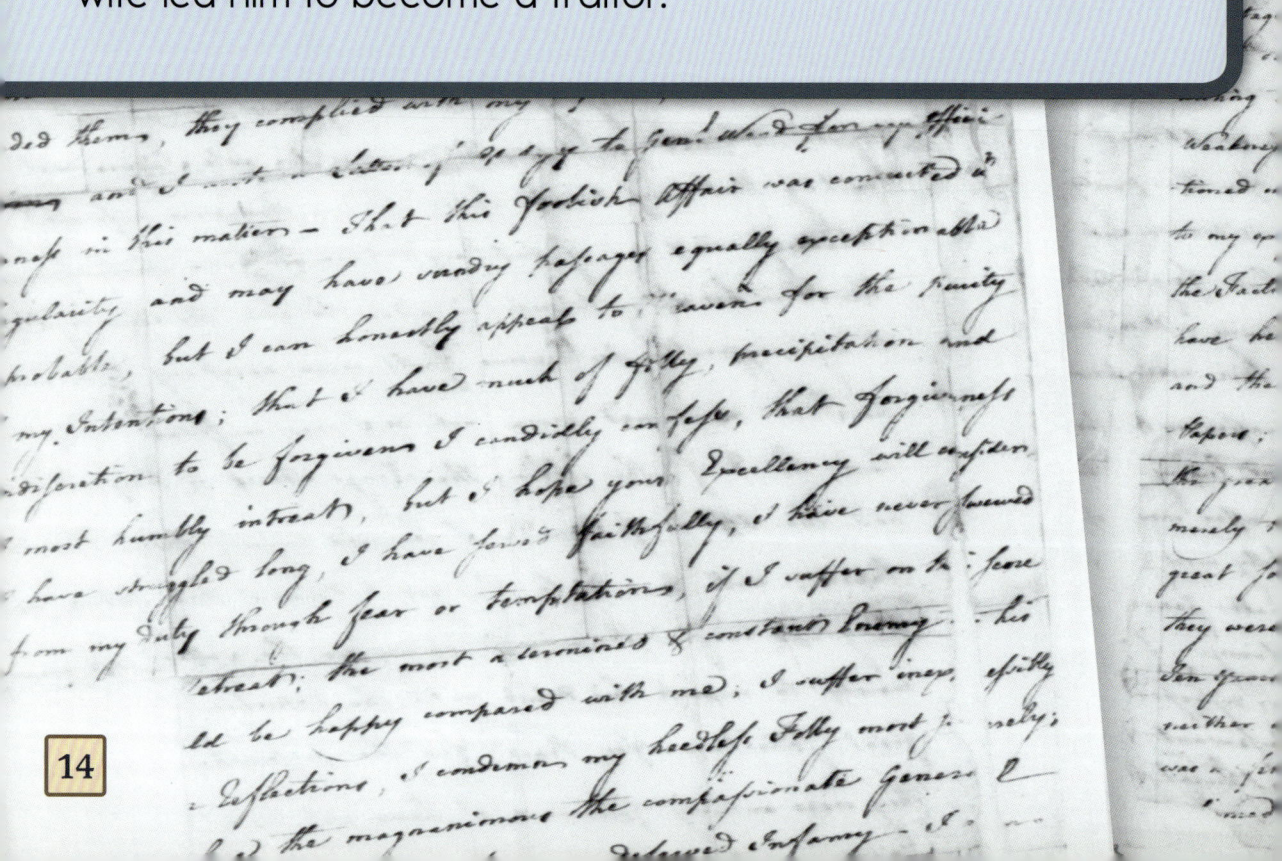

MORE TO EXPLORE

Under Benjamin's supervision, the **HENRY VASSALL HOUSE** became the headquarters of the army's medical department. Dr. Church was held here as a prisoner after people discovered he was a spy.

SPY WOMEN

Women could not serve in the military, but they found other ways to help the war effort. Some of them operated as spies. Both the American and British armies recruited women to work as cooks and maids. At the time, most men considered women innocent and nonthreatening. As a result, women could often come and go as they pleased. They were able to eavesdrop on soldiers' conversations, gather sensitive information, and pass it on to other spies.

Some women spied on the enemy in unusual ways. Anna Smith Strong, a member of the Culper Spy Ring, used her clothesline to signal other spies, hanging black petticoats to indicate that intelligence reports were available. She also hung handkerchiefs on the line to show where the hidden documents could be found.

MORE TO EXPLORE

The Culper Spy Ring used **SIX COVES** along the Long Island shore for dead drops. The number of handkerchiefs hanging on Anna's clothesline corresponded to the cove where the message was hidden.

MAP OF **LONG ISLAND**

British soldiers used the home of Lydia Barrington Darragh for meetings. She often served refreshments to the men or replenished wood in the fireplace, listening to their plans. Her husband recorded the information in shorthand, and then she placed the note under a cloth-covered button on her son's coat. Lydia's son carried the message to his older brother, who was serving in the army under George Washington.

British spy Ann Bates **DISGUISED HERSELF AS A PEDDLER** selling goods to soldiers. She gained access to George Washington's camp three times and gained valuable information about American troop and supply numbers.

WHO OUT-SPIED WHOM?

Revolutionary War spies on both sides worked hard to help their armies succeed. While they did not have the high-tech tools and resources that exist today, spies affected the outcomes of key battles. Ultimately, spies working for George Washington helped him win the war. As one British officer said, "Washington did not really outfight the British. He simply out-spied us."

GLOSSARY

cipher system
a secret or disguised way of sending a message

double agent
a spy pretending to serve one government while actually working for another

enlisted
joined the military

fortifications
structures built to protect places

lavish
expensive

munitions
military weapons

thwart
to stop someone from doing something

INDEX

Ann Bates 18
Anna Smith Strong 17
Battle of Yorktown 7
Benedict Arnold 12–13
Benjamin Church 14, 15
Benjamin Franklin 4
Benjamin Tallmadge 8–9
cipher system 10
Committee of Secret Correspondence 4, 5
Culper Spy Ring 8, 9, 10–11, 17
dead drop 10, 17
double agent 7
enlisted 6
fortifications 6
George Washington 6, 8–9, 12, 13, 18, 19
Henry Vassall House 15
invisible ink 10, 11, 13
James Armistead Lafayette 7
lavish 14
Lydia Barrington Darragh 18
munitions 2
Nathan Hale 6
spymaster 4, 8
thwart 2
women 16–17